the Anatomy of Nazism

by Earl Raab

Illustrated

Published by:
The Anti-Defamation League of B'nai B'rith
315 Lexington Avenue, New York, N. Y. 10016
in cooperation with
The Free Sons of Israel • 257 W. 93rd Street, New York, N.Y. 10025

Preface

For at least a quarter of a century it has been clear to a great many students of society that something new has appeared in the world—totalitarianism. Totalitarianism is industrialization plus tyranny plus mass organization plus ideological passion. It is the dark face of Industrial Man. It is not a thing of the past, but of the present. It may well be our future.

Hitler Germany was totalitarianism in its most virulent form. The Nazis made it unmistakably clear that the loss of political freedom can have the most dreadful consequences, not just for politicians, but for many millions of ordinary people. To many, the deeds of the Nazis were so shocking as to be beyond belief. Yet Nazism was not unique. It created a totalitarian state, a society in many essential ways similar to totalitarian communism.

A great deal has been written about totalitarianism. We have learned much about its appeal, its energies, its strategies, its consequences. We know, for example, that totalitarianism is more than a conspiracy of evil men. It represents one response to the problems of modern society, one way of mobilizing effort and overcoming resistance to change. During the 1930's the main problem was economic depression, especially widespread unemployment. Today another great problem dominates the scene—how to meet the demand of underdeveloped countries for rapid entry into the family of modern industrial states. Once again, totalitarianism offers its own answers and finds a ready response. It is a twice-told tale.

There is a real danger that what we have learned will not be effectively communicated, especially to young people. This pamphlet will help meet the need for educational materials that spell out the meaning of totalitarianism. While it concentrates on Nazism, it calls attention to the general totalitarian features of that movement and regime. Thus, guides are offered toward a better understanding of what lies behind today's headlines.

PHILIP SELZNICK
Professor of Sociology
University of California at Berkeley

CHAPTER I

THE BEGINNINGS OF NAZISM

On a cold September day in 1919, an unemployed handyman named Adolf Hitler joined an obscure political party of six members. Fifteen years later, he was the undisputed ruler of a nation of 66,000,000 people, and considered by many the most formidable figure in the world. Twelve years after that he ended his own life in a rubbled cellar, amid the wreckage of a world that would never be the same.

In those dozen turbulent years, the lives of 25,000,000 men, women and children were violently, deliberately snuffed out, many more millions were uprooted from their homelands; whole cities were destroyed, governments overturned, countries swallowed.

Never before had men killed each other and destroyed each other's cities and homes with such wholesale ruthlessness and ferocity. The wellspring of this mass destruction was not Hitler, but the Nazism which he helped to create. For Nazism was not just another political system. It was a total way of life. As a way of life, it was a systematic denial of those human values which the civilized man and the religious man have come to cherish. Yet Nazism sprang up in what was considered a highly civilized society, among men who were apparently reared with religious ideals. Nazism was not a simple throwback to the primitive ages; it was a clear product of the twentieth century, as one version of a social philosophy which still flourishes in this century.

This is how it happened: After World War I, the older political regimes of Europe fell like so many overripe apples. Some fell because of military defeat; others because of internal collapse under the pressure of war. An economic depression gripped Europe in the wake of the war and spurred the restless political movement. Many attempts were made to replace dislodged monarchies with constitutional governments modeled after those of the United States or Great Britain. But the idea was too alien, the times too unsettled, the demands too pressing for democracy to be able to sink its roots.

For example: Poland held its first general election under a democratic constitution in 1922; but in 1926 Marshal Pilsudski marched into the capital with troops, forced the resignation of the president and personally took over the reins of government. The constitution was then revised to fit his needs.

The Republic of Hungary was created in 1918; but in 1920, Admiral Horthy proclaimed Hungary a monarchy and himself Administrator of the Realm.

The people of Greece voted for the establishment of a republic in 1925. In 1926, General Galagos established a military dictatorship. Constitutional government was reestablished, but in 1935 the monarchy was restored, and in 1936 the constitution was suspended and dictatorial powers granted to General Metaxas.

And in two countries of Europe, the road away from monarchy —and then away from experimental constitutional government— took an even sharper turn.

Monarchy in Russia was overthrown in March of 1917. A provisional government was set up under a socialist coalition which promised constitutional liberties and drastic economic reforms. But in November, the Communists seized power and set up their own government. They won less than one-third of the seats in the election of a constituent assembly, but dispersed the majority with armed force. A controlled system of parliaments was established which was stripped of all power in 1925 when Josef Stalin took over. The Communist Party had become the state.

In Italy, the first general election under universal manhood suffrage was held in 1921. In the same year, a former newspaperman named Benito Mussolini founded the Fascist Party. A year later, he threatened a march on Rome, whereupon the king invited him to form a government. In 1925, opposition parties were formally dissolved. The Fascist Party had become the state.

Both the Fascist Party in Italy and the Communist Party in Russia established comprehensive systems of government aimed at maintaining tight control not only over the political life of their respective countries but over economic, social, and moral life as well.

Against this troubled backdrop the Nazi Party came to power in a Germany which, like the rest of Europe, was in a state of upheaval.

Germany considered the terms of the Versailles Treaty, which ended World War I, unjustifiably harsh and humiliating. She was officially saddled with "war guilt." Her war leaders were to be extradited for trial. She was barred from maintaining an army or navy. She was ordered to pay astronomically high amounts of money to the Allies for indemnity. Later, the indemnity figures were scaled down and virtually forgotten because Germany was never in a position to pay. The war leaders were never actually extradited. But the nation nevertheless smarted.

The postwar years were economically disastrous for Germany. An American dollar could buy about four German marks before the war—and about four trillion marks in 1923. While economic conditions became more stable for a brief period, Germany was hit hard by the general world depression. The number of unemployed swelled from about 2,000,000 in 1929 to about 4,500,000 in 1931, and to over 6,000,000 in 1933. Almost a quarter of all the working people in Germany were unemployed. In 1932 industrial production dropped to about half of what it had been in 1929.

And the German experiment in constitutional government—the Weimar Republic—had a number of strikes against it from the beginning. There had never been a democratic tradition in Germany. The rule of the Prussian nobility never had been seriously challenged. The Weimar Republic really had not been established as an expression of the desires of the German people, but had been virtually imposed by the Allies. It was a foreign import which never captured the allegiance of the Germans.

Against this background of economic suffering, "national humiliation" and political weakness the Nazi Party came to power.

Adolf Hitler joined the Nazi Party soon after its formation and almost immediately became its principal spokesman. There is no doubt that Hitler's bombastic personality strongly influenced the nature and success of the Nazi movement. He was born in a small border town near the Bavarian frontier, the son of a petty Austrian customs official. He apparently had a brooding resentment of his own which matched the mood of postwar Germany. A corporal in the wartime army, he dabbled in painting, and worked intermittently in the building trades, but never really found his calling until he joined the little political group of malcontents in Munich which became the National Socialist German Workers (Nazi) Party. There were many such groups springing up and dying in Germany. But this one did not die.

At the public meetings which the Nazis began to hold early in 1920, Hitler exhibited his talents as a rabble-rouser. He did not even have a high school education, and spoke simple, barely grammatical German. But he knew crowd psychology and the art of moving his audiences. He spoke hoarsely and hysterically, with pounding motions and burning eyes. He had the demagogue's talent of striking at the heart of the audience's desires, and telling them what

7

they wanted to hear. Almost 2,000 people came to the first large Nazi Party meeting in 1920 at which Hitler outlined the party's 25-point program. The program notably contained something for everybody except those who had to serve as the villains of the piece. He pledged, among other things: More land and territory for Germans; a nation in which only those of "German blood" would be full-fledged citizens; confiscation of war profits; old age pensions; low rentals to small businessmen; protection against Communism; abolition of interest on land and mortgages: protection of mothers and children; higher education for all qualifying Germans; a strong centralized state.

In making these promises, he whipped up the anger of his audiences against forces which he claimed were conspiring to keep Germany in its poverty-stricken state. The combination of easy promises and scapegoating proved an effective formula.

In 1921, the Nazi Party with branches in a few southern German towns had a membership of about 3,000. By 1923, the Party membership had grown to about 17,000. General Erich von Ludendorf of World War I fame, along with a few wealthy industrialists, had given his support to the movement. In November of 1923, the Nazis attempted what has come to be called the "Beerhall Putsch." Hitler interrupted a political meeting by firing two shots, jumping to a table and shouting: "The national revolution has broken out. The Bavarian government is deposed. The Reich government is deposed." This turned out to be something of an overstatement. The army quelled the "uprising" and Hitler and some of the Nazi leaders were tried for treason. Hitler, who delivered a four-hour harangue in court, was sentenced to five years' imprisonment, but was released after about a year—in 1925. In that year the Nazi Party had 27,000 members; in 1927, 72,000; in 1929, 178,000; in 1931, 862,000; and in 1932, well over a million.

Meanwhile, the Nazi Party was building up an octopus like apparatus with which it could control every aspect of national life. In 1932, there were 49 Nazi newspapers being published throughout Germany. A Nazi Youth Section had been established; a Nazi Woman's League; a Nazi Teachers' Association; a Nazi Physicians' Association; even a Nazi Association of Jurists.

After the failure of the "Beerhall Putsch" in 1923, the Nazis concentrated on getting elected to power by the people. Until 1930, the Nazi Party was not taken seriously by either the Germans or the foreign press, and was considered just another of many political splinter groups. But in 1930, the political and economic weaknesses of Germany reached a new crisis. The depression was at its worst.

The various parties in the national legislature—the Reichstag—could not agree on a policy or a cabinet. Many politicians felt that Hitler, once in power, would prove to be manageable. President Hindenburg, also a former German general, was forced to dissolve the Reichstag and order new elections.

The Nazi Party held over 30,000 meetings throughout the country and astonished the world by polling over 6,000,000 votes, second only to the Social Democratic Party, which drew over 8,000,000 votes. The next two largest groups, the Communist Party and the Central Party, polled about 4,000,000 votes apiece. Two years later, in the Reichstag election of 1932, the Nazi Party polled over 13,000,000 votes against 8,000,000 for the Social Democrats, becoming the largest party in Germany.

The political situation in the government deteriorated rapidly. The Nazis were the largest single party in the Reichstag, but not the majority. No chancellor appointed by President Hindenburg could get the majority support of the Reichstag, and finally, Hindenburg appointed Hitler to the position of chancellor. Hitler called another Reichstag election, and again failed to secure a clear Nazi majority.

The Nazis finally took direct action and refused to seat the delegates who had been elected on the Communist Party ticket. Now, with the support of a Prussian Party delegation, the Nazis had a majority in the Reichstag and promptly voted Hitler dictatorial powers. The year was 1933.

In 1934, Hindenburg died, and Hitler took over the powers of the presidency as well as the chancellorship. The German people were called upon to approve his taking of power in a popular referendum. In subsequent years all other political parties were outlawed, and the German voter was offered only one list of political candidates—the Nazi list. The Nazis had become the state.

They became even more than that. National life in its entirety was programmed by the Nazis. Labor, business, agriculture, children, women, religion, the courts and the law all were organized and controlled according to Nazi specifications. Opposition was crushed and concentration camps set up for the dissidents and for those whom the Nazis chose as whipping boys. Jews, the particular scapegoat-targets of the Nazis, although not the only ones, were deprived of their citizenship, their jobs, their freedom, and eventually their lives.

Meanwhile, the Nazis embarked on the program of military expansion which led to World War II. In 1936, German troops occupied a Rhineland zone which had been demilitarized after World War I. In March, 1938, German troops occupied Austria. In September, the Nazis demanded cession of part of Czechoslovakia to Germany. At an historic meeting in Munich, Britain and France futilely attempted to "appease" the Nazis by yielding to this demand in return for a "Peace Declaration." But treaties were so many scraps of paper to Hitler. In March, 1939, German troops occupied Bohemia and Moravia. On August 24, the Nazis signed a non-aggression pact with Russia, and one week later on September 1, invaded Poland.

This precipitated the general world-wide conflict which ended with the unconditional surrender of Germany in May, 1945. Hitler had committed suicide in his wrecked chancellery the month before. Over 8,000,000 men had been killed in combat. Over 8,000,000 men, women and children—Jews, Poles, Russians, and others—had been exterminated by the Nazis in gas chambers and by other means. Several million other civilians had died as a direct result of war. The losses in terms of homes, crops, industries were incalculable. Europe was in waste.

However, while two totalitarian regimes had been deposed—for the Italian Fascists went down with the Nazis—the totalitarian concept was far from dead. The military victory of the Allies did not necessarily mean the ideological victory of constitutional democracy. The opposing concepts of totalitarianism and democracy still wrestle with each other across the world—between nations and within nations. The Nazi regime offered a particularly revealing example of totalitarianism in thought and action. What was it about—and what was it like?

CHAPTER II

LIFE UNDER NAZISM

All the waking hours of the Germans were directed towards "service to the community," in ways prescribed by the Nazis. Such a schedule for 66,000,000 people required superorganization. Dr. Ley, head of the Labor Front, boasted: **"Our state never releases the human being from the cradle to the grave. We start with the child of three years: as soon as he begins to think, he is already given a little flag to carry. Thereafter follow school, Hitler Youth, S.A. (Nazi troops), military service. We do not let go of the human being and when all that is over, the Labor Front comes and takes him once more and does not let him go until he dies, whether he likes it or not."**

Youth and Education

The Nazis stripped the states and localities of all control over the schools. Parents' and teachers' organizations were abolished. Teachers' associations were disbanded, and all teachers required to join the Nazi teachers' association. All students' organizations were abolished and replaced by a German Student Corporation under the control of the Nazis. The courses of study were laid down by the Nazis, and designed to downgrade the intellect. The German Student Corporation decreed that a good political record is better than a good scholastic record. Hitler maintained that education must be aimed not at pumping in knowledge but at breeding absolutely healthy bodies.

The schools became propaganda mills. Here, for example, is a problem in a basic arithmetic text as prepared by the Nazis: **"The Jews are aliens in Germany. In 1933, there were 66,066,000 inhabitants in the German Reich, of whom 499,682 were Jews. What is the percentage of aliens?"**

Even fairy tales were revised for political purposes. The Nazi Teachers' Gazette published authorized versions of the Sleeping Beauty and Little Snow White. The Sleeping Beauty was to be regarded as Germany—and the Prince who awakened her with a kiss, Adolf Hitler.

But the Nazis went beyond the schools. They established an official youth organization, along military lines, to envelop the young people in their out-of-school hours. There were organizations of young people to include boys from the ages of 10-14, and girls of the same age. The Hitler Youth and the League of German Girls took over the boys from 14-18 and the girls from 14-21. All other youth organizations were abolished, and families that balked at letting their children join were considered suspect. The head of this youth apparatus, Baldur Von Schirach, said: **"Parents who prevent their sons from entering the Hitler Youth will be punished."** The Reich Master Craftsman warned the Germans: **"In the future no apprentice will be engaged who has not been a member of the Hitler Youth."**

The Hitler Youth had about 8,000,000 members between 14-18 in 1939. The program consisted mainly of pre-military training for the boys and pre-maternal training for the girls, plus Nazi indoctrination for all.

Hitler prophesied: **"If there are still people in Germany today who say—we will not join your community, we will remain as we are—then I reply: you will pass on but after you will come a generation that knows nothing else."**

Working Life

Businessmen, workingmen, and farmers were also organized like an army, to serve the needs of "the community."

Business life was regulated through a National Economic Chamber composed of divisions and sub-divisions representing different industries and also different regions. Every business was required to belong. In a sense, the German economy became one huge corporation with Hitler as chairman of the board.

Many large German industrialists had given financial support to aid Hitler in his rise to power, believing that he would save them from Communism. But after they achieved power, the Nazis made it clear that private industry was subservient to the state. Production had to follow lines laid down by the Nazis, and so did the use of corporate profits. Business, big and small, was tightly regimented. The president of the Reichsbank once confided that official communications made up more than one-half of the German manufacturers' entire correspondence. For example, in order to build a new boiler, the owner of one sugar refinery needed the permission of twelve different offices, to each of whom he had to supply multiple copies of all specifications. The head of one business estimated that he was subject to orders from 228 different government agencies.

It was the small businessman who suffered most dramatically —an ironic note, since the small businessmen, caught in the crush of the depression, provided most of Hitler's support in the early days. Part of the Nazi economic plan was the compulsory development of cartels—larger and larger amalgamations of businesses in any given industry. A cartel under one administrative head is easier to control than a number of scattered business firms. Cartelization—plus heavy taxation—plus the administrative burden of state control— plus the deliberate policies of the Nazis—drove out small business. As early as 1936, a Nazi newspaper reported that 18,000 hotel and restaurant owners had already been eliminated under the Nazi regime. Another Nazi newspaper reported in 1939 that in the previous three years, 180,000 handicraft businesses had been abolished. In the same year, the Nazis ordered 1,200 electrical firms to go out of business.

The farmers were similarly organized under a central Nazi agency called the Food Estate. Farmers were told what to produce, how much to produce, what techniques to use, where to market their produce, and what prices to charge. They even had to have permission from the state in order to take ownership of farms which they had inherited.

The workingmen of Nazi Germany also were mobilized by the Nazis. As soon as the Nazis took power, all labor unions were abolished. The Labor Front was established as an official state body which all employees had to join. But the Labor Front did not involve itself with questions of wages or working conditions. It was mainly concerned with providing indoctrination for the workers.

The "Leader" principle was officially applied to business life, and employers were empowered to fix wages and other conditions of employment, subject to the approval of the state. Strikes were prohibited. Workingmen were considered soldiers in the service of the Nazi community, and were not expected to think of their own material welfare. Robert Ley, head of the Labor Front, said to the workers of Germany: **"Formerly the soldier received twenty pennies. By this was clearly meant:'For your work as a soldier I cannot pay you nor does the Fatherland attempt to pay you for it. What it does do is provide you your nourishment, clothing and physical wellbeing.' Precisely in this sense are you a soldier."**

The worker could not choose his employment or change his employment without specific government permission; nor could he protest about the wages or other conditions of his employment; nor, as a final restriction, could he choose to be unemployed, since he was always subject to labor conscription. But what about his actual living standards?

Although employment rose from a low of 12,500,000 in 1933 to 22,000,000 in 1939, and average hourly earnings rose by 14 per cent, this rise reflected the massive efforts of a war economy. From the beginning, the Nazi economy concentrated on producing war material. Three-quarters of the increase in national production went to producers' goods—largely guns, bullets and other war-connected materials. Only one-quarter went to goods such as clothing, furniture and household appliances.

The state was prepared to purchase the war material as fast as it was produced, so the problems of relatively full production and employment were reduced. But the state could only purchase these goods by imposing heavy taxes on the citizens. In 1932, the German government was taking about 30 per cent of the national income in taxes. After five years of Nazi rule, the Germans' income tax went up to 47 per cent. The figure eventually reached almost 70 per cent.

The increase in employment and wages did not result in a substantially higher standard of living. Money wages barely kept up with the rise of prices caused by the shortage of goods. In 1936, despite increased employment, 13,000,000 Germans, or one out of five, still depended on state charity for the essentials of life. This they could depend on because even soldiers have to eat, but it was something less than "a decent standard of living."

Leisure Time

The ancient Roman emperors learned that when the bread supply is low, a spectacular circus might help to divert the people from their hunger. Nazi labor chief, Robert Ley, put it this way: **"We had to divert the attention of the masses from material to moral values. It is more important to feed the souls of men than it is to fill their stomachs."**

There was an additional reason for the Nazi state to engage heavily in leisure-time organization for the German people. This was another phase of daily life to be incorporated into the total system of state control. So, the Strength-Through-Joy movement was established, and placed under the control of the Labor Front. The leisure-time life of the population was carefully organized, again along army lines. Under the national office were 32 regional units, and under these units, 18,000 local groups. In the cities, there was a leisure-time block warden for every 25 persons. All recreational activities were incorporated in this organization, with departments

14

for culture, sports, travel, vacation. But all activities and entertainments were carefully controlled. The German citizen could see theatrical plays at low cost, but only those plays and actors that were approved by the Nazis. This government order was typical: **"In order to assure the penetration of the theatre with our Party philosophy, the Reich Theatre Chamber has given an order that in the future every theatre must employ eight actors and stage experts who are Party members."** The Reich Theatre Chamber was but one division of the Reich Culture Chamber which also had all-controlling departments of literature, radio, film, music, painting, and culture. Objectionable films, books, and art were simply destroyed so that nobody could see them. Goebbels held a public bonfire of tens of thousands of books, including the works of Freud, Zola, Proust, Einstein, Thomas Mann, H. G. Wells, Jack London, and many others.

It was difficult to find recreation, even in sports, that was uncontaminated by propaganda. The Nazis explained: **"All sports organizations must get instruction in politics and party philosophy. Non-political sport, so-called neutral sport, is unthinkable."**

It was often difficult to abstain from these recreational activities. One group of workers in Berlin received notices about an evening program in which "Our leader offers us a few enjoyable hours at a three-hour program of entertainment by professional artists." The invitation carried this sentence: **"It is the duty of every working comrade without exception to appear with his wife; exceptions can be allowed only if his wife is actually sick, a fact which must be proved in advance by presentation of a doctor's certificate when possible."**

Public Information and Expression

The only information and opinion which the German people could receive was that which was handed out to them by the Nazi Party. The success of political "double talk" and the "big lie" depended in large part on the absence of any expressions of fact or opinion which did not conform to Nazi doctrine. The Nazis immediately established a monopoly over the mass media, notably newspapers, films and radio. Within a year after the Nazis took power, 1,000 newspapers had been suppressed, and an additional 350 newspapers had voluntarily ceased publication. All newspapers were under the direction of the Reich Press Chamber, which had full power to censor them or to put them out of business. Goebbels said: **"The concept of the absolute freedom of press is definitely liberalistic and proceeds not from the people in its entirety but from the** individual . . . The more freedom of opinion that is conceded to an individual, the more it can harm the interests of an entire people."

In keeping with his dictate, the radio, theatre, libraries, and all other sources of information were censored as rigidly as the newspapers. No criticism of the basic policies of the government, or of its leaders, was permitted. Goebbels explained: **"The present government is perhaps not always right but no better government is conceivable."**

Neither was any group nor individual allowed to utter any dissent from or criticism of the government. Nazi law provided punishment for any statements "likely to undermine the confidence of the people in the political leadership." This meant, in effect, that a German was breaking the law if he expressed criticism of the government even to his own family over the breakfast table. The Hitler Youth were required to report such criticisms, and there were numerous cases of children reporting their own parents to the police.

Religion

In order to totally blanket the minds of the people, it was necessary for the Nazis to establish full control over all religious institutions. Not only did the Nazis consider organized religions as competitors, but they also believed that the pulpit was a channel for independent expression.

The Nazis first created a single state-sponsored Nazi Christian church to control and unify all of the Protestant congregations in Germany. An obscure minister who had long been sympathetic to the Nazis was established as "Reich Bishop" in charge of this national church. There were many Protestant ministers who opposed this maneuver and formed a League of Defense. In 1935, this group issued a statement warning against the "new heathenism." Over 700 Protestant ministers were immediately placed under arrest, and the Protestant churches were stripped of whatever authority they still had. Those who continued to speak out in criticism such as the heroic Pastor Martin Niemoller were arrested and imprisoned. Soon organized opposition became practically nonexistent.

Although the Nazis had signed a concordat with the Vatican in 1933 guaranteeing freedom of religious practice to Germany's 20,000,000 Catholics, this agreement was violated very quickly and with increasing frequency. The leader of Catholic Action was assassinated. The Catholic press was suppressed, the Catholic youth movement and educational system seriously harassed. Catholic priests and lay leaders were often arrested and imprisoned. Because of these developments, Pope Pius XI issued an anti-Nazi encyclical in 1937 which was read in the Catholic churches of Germany. Priests and nuns were arrested in large numbers, and new financial pressures were applied to the churches.

Because religious institutions were deeply rooted in Germany, it was not possible to abolish the churches overnight. But while the Nazis were attempting to suppress and subvert the churches, they were also engaged in weaning future generations away from Christianity. There was a long-range program to substitute a Nazi version for the traditional Christian religions.

One of the officials of the Nazi Christian Church said: **"We must get rid of the Old Testament. The Old Testament has rightly been called the most questionable book in the whole history of the world. It does not, cannot fit with a racially correct Christianity. A radical revision too must be made of the whole theology of the Rabbi Paul."**

A Nazi magazine commented on the Golden Rule in 1939: **"This fundamental law of Christianity completely contradicts our moral conscience, contradicts above all the warrior-like nature peculiar to the soul of our race."**

The children were taught to pray to Hitler instead of to God. Grace before meals given to the poor children by the Nazi Welfare Committee ended: **"For this food, my Fuehrer, my thanks I render."** Another official child's prayer ended: **"Fuehrer, my Fuehrer, my faith and my light, Heil my Fuehrer."**

Due Process of Law

Due process of law means that a person cannot be prosecuted without adequate proof that he actually violated the conditions of the law. It means that he must have an open court trial, with a jury if he so desires, in which he can bring in his own witnesses and challenge the witnesses against him. The Nazis exhibited complete contempt for due process. One of their first acts was to set up special "courts" for political offenses, in which no legal proof had to be offered in order for the judge to convict the accused. Indeed, a person could be retroactively convicted of a crime which had not been a crime at the time he committed it.

The Nazis carried this approach to its logical conclusion: the police were empowered to arrest, convict and punish people without any trial, and for any offenses they saw fit, whether a law was violated or not. The Nazi secret police, the Gestapo, was specifically authorized "to uncover and combat tendencies and developments

17

inimical to the state and to take to this end all measures deemed necessary and expedient." There was no check or control over its actions. Uncounted thousands of German citizens were arrested by the Gestapo and never seen again by their families.

Goering justified this Nazi contempt of the legal process in characteristic fashion: **"We do not recognize the exaggerated dictum that the law must prevail, even if everything collapses. We consider as a primary thing not the law but the people . . . there can only be one concept of the law: namely the one laid down by the Fuehrer . . . the law and the will of the Fuehrer are one."**

Representative Government

People vote in order to make choices—among parties, candidates or issues. If there are no choices open to them the vote becomes meaningless. The Nazis, after their assumption of power, removed all possibility of choice. All opposition parties were abolished. Any hint of opposition within the Nazi Party was crushed. When the German people voted on candidates, they were given only one candidate to vote for: the Nazi candidate. They could vote "yes" or "no" on this candidate, but the single candidates usually received the approval of over 99 per cent of the voters. Why? First of all, it was dangerous to vote "no." The Gestapo could—and often did—whisk away "no" voters without explanation or return. No one could criticize the actions of the government because freedom of speech was not permitted. The government could not be changed because there was no freedom of election. So by linking the one-party system to the abolition of free speech and press and to the abolition of due process, the Nazis had achieved a closed method of staying permanently in power. But, more than that, by establishing a monopoly on information and education, and using that monopoly skillfully, the Nazis apparently succeeded in "selling" the Nazi rule to large numbers of the German people.

Treatment of Human Beings

The Nazis deliberately used terror and brutality to maintain power and keep the population cowed. Organized brutality, besides being a political method for rooting out opposition, indicates a government's basic attitude toward human life and dignity. It reveals a fear and hatred of people. This basic hatred was at first unleashed toward Jews and non-Germans, and later turned against the Germans themselves.

The Nazis began their campaign against the Jews by restricting their movements, limiting their activities, and isolating them

18

from the German community. First, Jews were excluded from public office. Then they were prohibited from practicing such professions as law, medicine, and teaching. They were deprived of their citizenship and political rights. By January, 1939, no Jew could own or operate a retail or wholesale business, or pursue any independent occupation.

These were the economic and political measures that were most apparent to the eyes of the world. Meanwhile, other measures were being enforced for the sole purpose of demeaning and degrading the German Jews. They were forced to wear special identification; children were urged to jeer at them in the streets; they were prohibited from marrying non-Jews; and non-Jews who had social relations with Jews were subject to severe penalties.

But brutality, once unleashed, accepts no boundary lines. Degradation spilled over into physical attack. On November 10, 1938, for example, a telegram was sent by the Gestapo to all police bureaus stating that "spontaneous" anti-Jewish demonstrations were about to take place during the next several days and that the police should stand by for "the speedy jailing of the Jews." According to a report to Goering, the first night 191 synagogues were demolished, 171 Jewish homes set on fire, 20,000 Jews arrested and 36 assassinated by Nazi mobs. The records of Buchenwald Concentration Camp (mass prison), show that 10,000 Jews were received there between November 10-13. They were beaten and tortured while the Buchenwald loudspeakers repeated over and over: "Any Jew who wants to hang himself is asked to please put a piece of paper with his number in his mouth so that we may know who he is."

Such concentration camps became a standard part of the Nazi regime. As the Nazi armies took over Middle Europe and Poland, concentration camps sprang up throughout the continent, and millions of Jews were forced into them. After the war ended, the leading Nazis went on trial for their crimes against humanity. A special commission consisting of some of the world's outstanding jurists was set up in Nuremburg to examine witnesses and gather and sift documentary evidence relating to Nazi brutality.

The trials brought to light acts of calculated brutality and degradation unequaled anywhere in history. Here is a typical account by a German eyewitness of what happened to one group of Jews in a field in Poland on October 5, 1942:

"The people from the trucks—men, women, and children —were forced to undress under the supervision of an SS (Nazi Storm Trooper) soldier with a whip in his hand . . . I saw a pile of shoes, about 800-1000 pairs, great heaps of underwear and clothing. Without weeping or crying out these people undressed and stood together in family groups, embracing each other and saying goodbye . . . During the fifteen minutes I stayed there, I did not hear a single complaint or a plea for mercy. I watched a family of about eight: a man and woman about fifty years old, surrounded by their children of about one, eight and ten, and two big girls about twenty and twenty-four. An old lady, her hair completely white, held the baby in her arms, rocking it and singing it a song. The infant was crying aloud with delight. The parents watched the group with tears in their eyes. The father held the ten-year-old boy by the hand, speaking softly to him; the child struggled to hold back his tears. Then the father pointed a finger to the sky and stroking the child's head, seemed to be explaining something. At this moment the SS near the ditch called something to his comrade. The latter counted off some twenty people and ordered them behind the mound. The family of which I have just spoken was in the group. I still remember the young girl, slender and dark, who, passing near me, pointed to herself, saying 'twenty-three.' I walked around the mound and faced a frightful common grave . . . The ditch was two-thirds full. I estimate that it held a thousand bodies."

But the Nazis soon developed harsher means for the policy of genocide which they had officially adopted early in World War II. Under the direction of a special Nazi department headed by Adolf Eichmann, special chambers for mass execution by gas were built. Rudolf Hoess, the commander of one concentration camp, Auschwitz, boasted: **"We built our gas chambers to accommodate 2,000 people at a time."** He added: **"We knew when the people were dead because their screaming stopped."** The bodies were cremated in vast ovens; at Auschwitz, a record was set in June 1944 of 22,000 incinerations in 24 hours.

Altogether, 6,000,000 Jews were killed by these and other means. But these facilities were used for others as well. The Nuremberg documents indicated that close to 3,000,000 Poles and other non-Jewish Middle Europeans were also exterminated in this fashion.

The process of brutalization did not end with the mass murders themselves. Large quantities of soap were manufactured from the corpses of those murdered. The wife of one concentration camp commander had lampshades made of human skin. At another camp, mattresses were made of human hair. At another, children were

20

The post World War I years were economically disastrous for Germany. The Nazi Party came to power against a troubled backdrop of economic distress and political anarchy.

Marines join forces with workers to keep order in Berlin after World War I.

Aging President Hindenburg appointed Adolf Hitler to the position of Chancellor, although he did not get a clear majority of the votes cast in 1933.

Hitler had become identified with the Nazi Party from the beginning. At thousands of Nazi meetings held all over Germany he had displayed his talents as a rabble-rouser.

Brown Shirt Census

When Hitler became Chancellor, he assumed the mantle of absolute leader or "fuehrer." All political opposition was ruthlessly stamped out.

The Nazis became the state. The octopus-like apparatus they had
built up controlled every aspect of national life.

The Nazis established an official youth organization along military lines, to envelop the young people in their out-of-school hours.

Robert Ley: "Our state never releases the human being from the cradle to the grave."

The schools became propaganda mills which glorified militarism. This page from a primer urged children to round up their friends to salute the Nazis.

Automatic Reaction

All media of communication were rigidly controlled. A cartoonist comments on the muzzling of the German press.

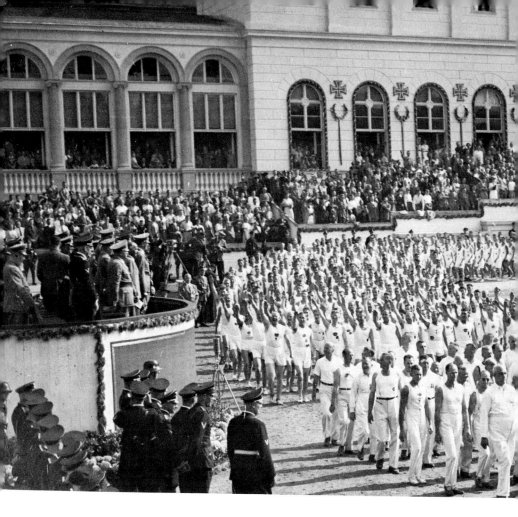

Even sports and leisure time life was directed and carefully organized by the Nazis. This photo depicts a sports tournament.

Nazi Propaganda Minister Goebbels held a public bonfire of tens of thousands of books that the Germans were forbidden to read.

A worker could not choose to leave his job . . . He could not even choose to be unemployed since he was always subject to labor conscription.

The Nazi philosophy stressed the concepts of authority and politics as religion.

To promote their philosophy, the Nazis used the techniques of double talk, the Big Lie and scapegoating.

The Jews were the primary scapegoat-targets of the Nazis. At first they were restricted by laws and publicly humiliated.

But brutality once unleashed accepts no boundary lines . . . They
were soon herded into mass concentration camps.

Millions of both Jews and non-Jews were gassed and their bodies
burned in ovens like these found at Dachau.

After violating a number of international treaties, Hitler, in
1939, unleashed the most destructive war in history.

Ruthless force brought millions of unwilling victims under Nazi domination.

Hitler had promised the Germans world domination. He brought only destruction and defeat. German refugees whose homes had been destroyed fleeing Aachen.

With defeat close at hand, Hitler ended his own life in a rubbled cellar, amid the wreckage of a world that would never be the same. A workman shovels the last moundful of dirt over the ruins of Hitler's suicide bunker.

"I did it to assure your destiny."

A cartoonist comments on Hitler's "accomplishments."

After the German defeat in 1945, Nazi leaders went on trial for their crimes against humanity. Herman Goering on left, next to Rudolf Hess.

Nazism's monuments . . . are the now empty gas chambers and crematoria at Dachau and Buchenwald. The inscription on this memorial at Dachau reads: "To honor the dead and admonish the living."

injected with tuberculosis germs and frozen to death in "medical experiments." One camp commander made bets on how long a human being could live hanging by his feet.

In 1938, a number of years before these events came to world attention in such detail, before the mass murders were perpetrated, commenting only on the repressive activities of the Nazi regime, President Franklin D. Roosevelt had said: "I myself could scarcely believe that such things could occur in a twentieth century civilization."

But this total "way of life"—from regimented education to mass murder—was not an historical freak; it flowed naturally from the ideals and guiding philosophies of Nazism as they were so clearly laid down.

CHAPTER III

NAZI PHILOSOPHY: Downgrading the Individual

Totalitarianism is not just a tongue-twisting synonym for dictatorship. The personal military dictatorships of General Pilsudski in Poland, or of Admiral Horthy in Hungary did not offer a full-blown theory of government to substitute for that of blood-line monarchy or of constitutional democracy. Nazism did offer such a theory, as did Fascism and Communism.

1—Accent on THE COMMUNITY

The collective community—rather than the individual—is supreme. Therefore, the political state (which is the arm of the community) is supreme.

Individuals are only cells in a higher social organism—the community—and are not important in themselves. Individuals are important only to the extent that they contribute to the welfare of the community. Hitler wrote that his goal was "the preservation and fostering of a community of living beings who are physically and mentally alike."

The means to that goal is the state or government which is the community's mechanism for controlling the individual. Where the community is all important and the individual without importance in himself, the state's power to control the individual "for the sake of the community" is therefore unlimited and absolute. A leading Nazi legal authority wrote: **"There are no personal liberties of the individual which fall outside of the realm of the state and which must be respected by the state . . . there can no longer be any question of a private sphere free of state influence . . ."**

The Nazis drew freely from the writings of political philosophers when they expressed views which fit in with their own. Hegel wrote: **"Everything that man is, he owes to the state . . . all value which man has, all spiritual reality he only has through the state."** King Frederic William I of Prussia summarized this philosophy very simply: **"In affairs of state, the good of the whole always** takes precedence over the good of the individual." The community thus takes on a kind of existence of its own which has little to do with the **people** who live in it at any given time. A rough analogy may be found in the case of a military regiment. The soldiers are units in that regiment and serve their function as soldiers only insofar as they contribute to the success of their regiment. In the course of a war, the personnel of that regiment may have had a 100 per cent turnover, but it still maintains its identity and its tradition as a regiment. The "good of the regiment" may not mean the same as the "good" of the soldiers in that regiment.

According to this approach, the community finally becomes an idea, a tradition, rather than a group of people. Not only is a single individual less important that the community, but all the individuals together are less important than the community just as the soldiers are less important than "the regiment." In practical terms, this means the elimination of the "individual" as such and the creation of "people-units" who are, in Hitler's words, "physically and mentally alike."

2—Accent on AUTHORITY
The state should be run by a leadership elite with absolute authority over the people, while acting "in the interests of" the community.

One Nazi leader, Otto Gauweiler, wrote: **"The [Nazi] Party stands above and beside the state as the wielder of an authority derived from the people . . . The legal position of the party is therefore that of a completely sovereign authority."**

The Nazis held the theory that they had received a mandate to act in the interests of the community; and their authority to act was absolute and boundless. Since the Nazi Party knew what was good for the community, there was no need for opposing parties or for parliamentary debate. Indeed, such opposition could only hamper the progress and efficiency of the community.

By further extension, the Nazi Party itself was led by a super-elite culminating in "Der Fuehrer"—Adolf Hitler—which had the same absolute authority. Robert Ley said: **"The National Socialists believe in Hitler who embodies their will . . . Only what Adolf Hitler, our Fuehrer, allows, or does not allow is our conscience."**

Nazi Party membership was restricted to ten per cent of the population, and each Party member took the following oath: "I promise at all times to respect and obey the Fuehrer and the leaders whom he appoints over me."

The implications of this "leadership" principle were carefully spelled out:

"... that the will of the people is embodied in the Fuehrer does not exclude the possibility that the Fuehrer can summon all members of the people to a plebiscite [vote] on a certain question. In this asking of the people the Fuehrer does not, of course, surrender his decisive power to the voters. The purpose of the plebiscite is not to let the people act in the Fuehrer's place or to replace the Fuehrer's decision with the result of the plebiscite. Its purpose is rather to give the whole people an opportunity to demonstrate and proclaim its support of an aim announced by the Fuehrer."

This principle was applied to formal political bodies as well:

"It would be impossible for a law to be introduced and acted upon in the Reichstag which has not originated with the Fuehrer or at least received his approval. The procedure is similar to that of the plebiscite. The law-giving power does not rest in the Reichstag; it merely proclaims through its decision its agreement with the will of the Fuehrer who is the law-giver of the German people."

Nazi theoreticians did not admit that this "leadership principle" ignored the will of the community. They insisted that the majority of the people were in support of their policies—but also insisted that these policies were best for the community and would be followed, even if the majority were to disagree. Indeed, it was the Nazi Party—and ultimately the Fuehrer—who unerringly understood the needs of the community, even when the majority of the people didn't. Herman Goering put it simply: "We National Socialists believe that in political affairs Adolf Hitler is infallible." This "infallibility" was not a light figure of speech but was meant literally.

3—Accent on THE "SELECT"

The community whose interests are to be served by its leaders does not include everybody—but is a special community selected by some higher law to fulfill a special destiny in the scheme of things.

German rulers and philosophers had for years been telling the Germans that they were a superior race. The Nazis built upon this legacy of extreme nationalistic pride. They quoted Count Keyserling, who wrote: "The German people who destroyed the old world were rough and cruel but they were also courageous, loyal and ready to sacrifice; this enabled them, given their talents, to be continuously better in the course of centuries, whereas Greeks and

24

Romans who were refined and false, perished through degeneration."

They quoted such writers as Houston Stewart Chamberlain who wrote: "**The races of mankind are markedly different in the nature and also in the extent of their gifts, and the Germanic races belong to the most gifted group, the group usually termed Aryan.**"

Thus, the Nazis maintained not only that the German community was superior, but that it was superior by the **inherited** nature of its people. Moreover, the Nazis held that this "natural superiority" of the German community meant that it was destined eventually to "lead" the world. This idea was embodied in the slogan Hitler used to tantalize the Germans: "**Today Germany, tomorrow the world.**"

Point 4 of the Nazi Party program read: "**None but members of the nation Volk [folk] may be citizens of the state. None but those of German blood, whatever their creed, may be members of the nation.**"

The Nazi theory thus ran in this circle:

- The **Volk** "of German blood" constituted the community;
- This community had an historic destiny and identity of its own, over and above the people who happened to live in it at any given time;
- The Nazi Party and the Fuehrer were the mystically selected instruments for directing this mystically selected community towards its destiny, and therefore had a higher mandate than even the expressed will of the people. Goebbels said: "**The great leader will not be elected, he is there when he must be there.**"
- Finally, to complete the circle, the Fuehrer even has the absolute power to arbitrarily decree who is and who is not "of German blood."

4—Accent on POLITICS AS RELIGION
The theory of a "sacred" community and its "sacred" leadership is offered as a religious system, complete with moral code, to substitute for other religious systems.

Nazism, with this mystique of **Volk** and blood and Fuehrer was obviously competing with other specific religious commitments. Hitler said: "**We wish for no other God than Germany.**" Baldur Von Schirach, head of the Nazi youth movement, said: "**I am neither a Catholic nor a Protestant; I am a National Socialist.**"

Hitler's role necessarily became "religious" in character: He

25

himself, commented, "I regard myself as the instrument of Providence." And Nazi leader Julius Streicher was less restrained: "It is only on one or two exceptional points that Christ and Hitler stand comparison, for Hitler is far too big a man to be compared with one so petty."

More significantly, perhaps, Nazism and its dictates were considered the ultimate and only test of morality. The aim as stated by one Nazi leader was to educate the German youth in such a manner that it doesn't learn anything that is not in harmony with National Socialism. It was as simple as that. Nothing was to be considered "wrong" or immoral which was done in the name of the higher cause of Nazism. And any act or thought that opposed Nazism was by definition immoral. For example, Alfred Rosenberg wrote: "A future German Reich will never accept a woman without children—it does not matter whether she is married or not—as a full member of the community of people. Consequently, adultery on the part of the man, in so far as offspring result therefrom, should not be made subject to legal prosecution."

The missionary nature of the Nazi "religion" was expressed in a German primer published in 1936: "The concept of the Reich is based on the idea that the whole civilized world must be united under a single power. The Reich incorporates a higher moral principle which directs the fate of the world, bringing order and justice. The Reich must direct the life of nations, individuals and states. The Reich signifies a mission."

The elements of Nazi philosophy were systematically drilled into every German. Since their philosophy stressed the emotional and irrational, the Nazis had to devise specific techniques to quell any analytical or rational approach to life.

CHAPTER IV

NAZI TECHNIQUES: Downgrading the Intellect

The Nazis were shrewd students of mass psychology and laid heavy emphasis on the techniques of manipulating crowds. All of the techniques they used served to promote and to inculcate their basic theories.

1—Accent on THE EMOTIONAL

Nazi programs and techniques were characterized by their emotional appeal. There was a heavy use of symbolism and dramatic pomp. Hitler himself chose the swastika, "the hooked cross" of ancient vintage as the official symbol of the Nazi Party. It became part of the national flag, Party members wore it on armbands, it provided a huge backdrop for the mass rallies which the Nazis frequently held. A special stiff-arm salute was devised and exchanged at every opportunity, often accompanied by the official Nazi cry, "Heil Hitler!" The mass meetings were expertly staged extravaganzas in lighting and ritual, with thousands of voices shouting in unison "Sieg Heil! Sieg Heil!" over and over again with hypnotic and apparently exhilarating effect.

There was a more explicit anti-intellectual emphasis: an impatience with any "thinking" or "weighing of considerations" which might get in the way of direct action. Herman Goering said: **"I am not concerned with both sides. I see only those who are for National Socialism and those who are against it, and I know how to deal with the latter."**

There was impatience with people who spent their time thinking and weighing when they could be "doing" things for the community. Hitler said: **"A young man who works with a spade for six months on the Western fortifications has done more for Germany than an intellectual has done during his whole life."**

There was a constant emphasis on force as distinct from reflection, and an equation of military force with national strength. Alfred Rosenberg wrote: **"The measure of the strength of a people is always and exclusively its readiness for military conflict."**

27

This Nazi appeal to direct action, uncluttered by the need to think or evaluate, was obviously meant to attract large sections of the restless German population, and particularly the youth. It was summed up by the chief architect of Nazi propaganda, Joseph Goebbels, in these words: "**National Socialism has simplified the thinking of the German people and led it back to its original primitive forms.**"

2—Accent on "DOUBLE TALK" and "THE BIG LIE"

Propaganda for the purpose of influencing masses is one of the means the Nazis used to maintain their control. They recognized that political control of a modern nation could not be maintained by force alone. Substantial mass support was needed, even while parliamentary democratic forms were being abandoned. The Nazi program was so worded that it appealed to the hopes and desires of the people even when their actions were flouting these desires; they used appeals to patriotism; they flattered the people by telling them they belonged to a superior race; and they provided scapegoats and alibis for past failures.

The idea behind political "double talk" is to mask undemocratic actions by insisting that they are **really** the most democratic in the long run; or to mask warlike actions by insisting that they are **really** the most peaceful in the long run. At the least, this technique helped to blur a number of basic issues.

For example, on the subject of democracy, Nazi leader Rudolf Hess said: "**Not the so-called democracies, no, we, the so-called dictatorship, the country with the authoritarian regime, we have made the goal of a free nation law and thereby we have done the most democratic deed.**"

Dr. Frick, Nazi Minister of the Interior, stated flatly: "**It is silly to claim that National Socialism governs by a dictatorship. The government of the Fuehrer in Germany is the most genuine and the purest democracy of the world.**"

In the midst of troop movements across borders, Hitler proclaimed from a public platform: "**No European state has done more for peace than Germany. None has made greater sacrifices for peace.**"

In the midst of Nazi-organized physical attacks on German Jews, the leader of the Nazi "faith movement" declared: "**The intolerance of Christianity is typically unGerman while tolerance for people of other creeds is typical of us Germans.**"

In part this technique involved a subtle reshaping of the meaning of common words. One Nazi magazine editorialized: **"The Vikings once conquered a town in England. The men lay slain. The women were made slaves. There remained only children, without use and without future. What did they do, these true humanitarians? They threw the children into the air and caught them on the points of their spears. The Vikings were truly merciful."** This "act of mercy" was made to sound reasonable by quietly slipping in a few completely unwarranted assumptions: that the children were without use, or that it was necessary to kill the men and enslave the women in the first place. Such words as "democracy," "peace" and "humanitarianism" have been called "glittering generalities" when used without analysis, and the Nazis were masters at adapting such words to their own purposes.

Of course, part of the Nazi propaganda technique was simply the art of fabrication. Hitler wrote: **"A definite factor in getting a lie believed is the size of the lie. The broad mass of the people, in the simplicity of their hearts, more easily fall victim to a big lie than to a small one."**

Before Austria was invaded, Hitler said publicly: **"The assertion of the Austrian government that from the side of the Reich an attack would be undertaken or planned I must emphatically reject."**

While plans were made to invade Bohemia, Moravia and Poland, Hitler asserted: **"We have assured all our immediate neighbors of the integrity of their territory as far as Germany is concerned. That is no hollow phrase; it is our sacred will."**

After the invasion took place, the Nazis found the words to explain that conditions, not Nazi principles, had unfortunately changed. According to Hitler: **"Czechoslovakia broke up not because Germany desired her breakup, but because it is impossible to construct and uphold around the conference table artificial states."**

Goebbels put it bluntly when he said: **"We have made the Reich by propaganda."**

3—Accent on SCAPEGOATING

Nazi philosophy and Nazi technique blended at the point where whole human groups were excluded from the "select community," blamed for all the community's problems, and persecuted for their alleged crimes.

Jews were the primary scapegoat-targets of the Nazis. They were a "convenient" target group. There was a European and a specifically German tradition of using Jews as scapegoats. This tradition stretched back to the religious animosities of the Middle

29

Ages when the Jews refused to abandon their ancient faith even in the face of the most severe penalties. They were often killed and, as a group, thrust out of the community; barred from most occupations; removed from the land; and, in the larger cities, confined in separate, walled quarters known as ghettos. This policy was officially abandoned after the French Revolution. The official emancipation of German Jewry began after Napoleon invaded Germany, but many of the attitudes sustained by the centuries-old ghetto walls did not crumble overnight, and new fears were fanned by ultra-nationalists. During the nineteenth century, the Germans became conscious of themselves as a nation. The humiliating defeats at the hand of Napoleon caused a defensive reaction, and nationalistic feeling ran high. Everything German was extolled; everything "foreign" was denounced. The Jews, because of their religious traditions which harked back to an ancient land, Israel, and because a number of them were liberal and had a cosmopolitan outlook, became associated with the foreign. This, despite the fact that they considered themselves patriotic Germans, and many fought and died in the German army.

Jews were disproportionately forced to find their livelihood in "self-employed" vocations; and were largely restricted to the professions, and to the "fringe" and "new" enterprises, such as retail business, entertainment and communications industries. Few were landowners and few were permitted to enter governmental service or achieve high rank in the military. The Jews thus tended to become a part of the growing middle class in the German economy.

As a result, in the Germany of the 1870's which was afflicted with economic distress and political tension, many political groups found it possible to divert popular unrest into animosity toward the Jews. They did this by assigning the Jews roles calculated to arouse the antagonism of different classes. For the farmers, the Jews were made the hated symbols of urbanism; for the pinched middle class, the symbols of competition; for workers, the symbols of the middle class; for the aristocracy, the symbol of social change. By 1893, there were sixteen deputies in the German Parliament who had been elected on a frankly anti-Semitic platform. It was during this period that a German journalist invented the term "Anti-Semitism," to refer specifically to the deliberate stimulation and use of anti-Jewish prejudice for political purposes.

The Nazis further extended this tradition by establishing the myth of the Jew as some kind of distinct biological "race": it fit "nicely" with the Nazi theories about the "German race" itself. And within this network of theories about "inferior" and "superior"

30

races lay the Nazis' most comprehensive use of the techniques of fabrication and "double talk."

The Myth of Race

The Nazis spoke of the superiority of the "Aryan race" with which they identified the German people, and the inferiority of the "Jewish race." However, the following facts have long been common knowledge and were re-emphasized by some of the world's scientists in a statement released by the United Nations in 1950:

a) Race is a term of convenience used by anthropologists to loosely describe human groups which have relative concentrations of certain physical characteristics because of geographical isolation. Thus, there is general agreement in roughly classifying mankind into three major "racial" divisions: Mongoloid, Negroid, and Caucasoid because of certain statistical differences in physical characteristics.

b) However, this anthropological term has no relationship to innate mental characteristics, temperament, personality, or character; or to "superiority" or "inferiority" on any level.

c) Even if the term were only applied to physical characteristics, there is no "German" (or Nordic) race. Germans are a nationality, like Americans and Frenchmen, Liberians, Mexicans, Israelis, and Canadians.

d) Even if the term were only applied to physical characteristics, there is no "Jewish" race. Jews, like Catholics, Protestants, and Moslems, are a religious group, with certain historical and cultural traditions.

e) "Aryan" does not describe race, nationality, religion or anything else on the face of the earth, except perhaps a kind of language root which most of the western world shares. The existence of the "Aryan" race is the purest of fictions.

Nevertheless, the Nazis sold the German people their "Aryan vs. non-Aryan" myth by repeating it often enough, not brooking any counter-statements, and making it appealing for the German people to hear. The obvious contradictions were dealt with simply by adapting the facts to the pre-conceived system. For example, in supporting the idea that Germanic Aryans have always been leaders, the Nazis "discovered" that great men like Dante, Marco Polo, Michelangelo, Bacon, Lavoisier, and Louis IV were actually German Aryans, and that the ancient Egyptians and Greeks had Nordic blood.

And, finally, of course, as befits a "religious" system, contradictions were accepted "on faith," without question. The "superior

Aryan" was supposed to be blond, tall and slim, even though the "most superior Aryan," Adolf Hitler, was himself markedly brunette; his lieutenant, Goering, as round as a beer barrel; and his other lieutenant, Goebbels, dark and dwarfish.

The Myth of Conspiracy

The Nazis had a simple explanation for all domestic and international problems. Why did Germany lose World War I? Why was there widespread unemployment? Why was the tuberculosis rate high? All of the difficulties and failures of Germany were blamed on a conspiracy of the Jews. Often contradictions appeared, but the Nazis never felt any need to account for them. The Jews were called the international bankers of the world, and at the same time called the international communists of the world. One Nazi pamphlet announced: **"The Jew as dictator of democracy, Bolshevism and the Vatican, rules over all of you."** Julius Streicher once told the medical officers of Germany: **"The Jews have taught the Germans to smoke tobacco in order to destroy the German nation."**

In short, the Jews were the symbols of everything that was frustrating or evil. The target of this Nazi propaganda was not any specific Jew at all, but a myth of **The Jew** which had been fabricated. But a scapegoat needs to be flogged to serve its purpose of releasing anger and frustration—and since a myth cannot be satisfactorily flogged, the flesh-and-blood Jews were. **"On each telegraph pole from Munich to Berlin we must display the head of a prominent Jew,"** declared Rosenberg in 1933, before the Nazi program became even more ambitious.

The scapegoating technique was established and carried to its ultimate extreme with the Jews, but it did not stop there. It became a convenient technique to be applied also against any group which maintained its own identity or resisted the brutality of Nazism. The Roman Catholic Church, for example, was a favorite target. One Hitler Youth Proclamation warned: **"Do you notice the Roman clerical bloodsuckers? Therefore, German youth, keep away and form a distinct front against Catholics and Jews, those international criminals."** Nazi leader Ammerlahn explained: **"Roman Catholics are the black vultures of German nationalism and the drummers of discord in the German nation. We will not stop until we have scratched them out of the lives of the German people."**

The freemasons soon joined the list of organizational enemies and so did all of the church institutions, Protestant or Catholic, which threatened Nazi supremacy by their very existence.

The striking characteristic of these various techniques is that they are so in keeping with the basic Nazi beliefs. Only when the individual human being is downgraded and considered nothing more than a number can he be treated with the contempt that such obvious distortions denote. And, on the other hand, it was by the effective use of such propaganda that the Nazis were able to blunt the intellects of so many people and reduce them, in fact, to statistics rather than individual people.

CHAPTER V

TOTALITARIANISM AND DEMOCRACY

In summary, Nazism can be described from several different vantage points:

• *As Anti-Humanism*—The individual is debased, and the dignity and value of human life is debased. Brutality becomes a way of life, a way of life that is encouraged and extolled.

• *As Anti-Intellectualism*—The human mind and human reason are ridiculed and debased. The physical and the emotional are glorified.

• *As a Parody of Democracy*—Everything is done "in the name of the people." Everything is justified as "the will of the people." The people are constantly addressed by radio, by newspaper, by mass meetings, and group meetings. Mass involvement in government organizations and activities is required. There are even controlled elections and referenda to approve government policies. All the forms and surface language of democracy are used—but it is only a "pretend-democracy" because all of these "popular" activities and involvements are rigidly directed from above.

• *As a means of "Permanent" Control*—The regime can be overthrown only by force. But at the same time the regime has concentrated all force in its own hands. Furthermore, the regime controls all the instruments of information and education, so that it is impossible to foment discontent or revolt.

• *As Total State Power*—The scope of the government's power is **total** and unlimited; and its control over the individual is **total** and unlimited. The individual is under the direct control of his government in his work, in his play, in his education, in his church, in his neighborhood, and even in his family. There is no place to hide—no privacy. The Party-State reaches everywhere, and has absolute power over everything.

"Total power" is, of course, the characteristic which is uniquely at the heart of Nazism. Anti-humanism and anti-intellectualism are inevitable results, as well as the basic philosophical ingredients of

34

total state power. It is through such total power that permanent political control is achieved. And total power which tries to make use of democratic forms must parody democracy.

In other words, where there is total state power, there is "permanent" political control, anti-humanism, anti-intellectualism, and a parody of democracy. All of these elements are tied up in one package which we refer to as "totalitarianism." It is a descriptive package which can be applied to any totalitarianism, whether it is known as Nazism, Communism, or any other name.

However, because they depend for their initial appeal on popular support, totalitarian regimes would never accept these negative descriptions. They would deny that they are anti-human, anti-intellectual or anti-democratic. Indeed, they claim that they are the "true" democracies, that they unerringly represent the wishes of the masses. How are they, then, revealed?

They are revealed, of course, by their deeds, but these are not always easy to discover and by the time they are discovered it is often too late. They are revealed most sharply by their philosophic accents—and then by their techniques. The exact methods and ideals of all totalitarian systems are not identical and interchangeable—any more than are the different systems of democracy. But their basic accents are the same.

Thus Communism, although differing from Nazism in specific ideological content, shares with Nazism certain of the basic accents we have discussed. Communism, like Nazism, stresses the primacy of the community over the individual; it places a high value on the "select" community of the trained Communist vanguard; it demands obedience to authority, and it substitutes politics for religion. Like Nazism, Communism uses the techniques of scapegoating and the Big Lie to maintain an image of mass appeal.

How do the accents of totalitarianism and democracy compare?

1—Accent on community vs. accent on the individual. In a democracy, the community exists solely for the purpose of helping the individuals in the community to fulfill themselves. In the community people can work together to fulfill their individual purposes. The state's power is limited. It does not have the power to interfere with the basic rights of the individual, even if the majority would desire such interference. The individual is limited only by the rights of other individuals. The American Bill of Rights, for example, spells out these basic, inviolable rights. They are not granted by the state, because these rights are considered natural rights—rights with which a person is born. The state exists to

35

protect those rights. Thomas Jefferson wrote: **"The freedom and happiness of man are the sole objects of all legitimate government."**

2—Accent on authority vs. accent on expressed will. The accent in a democracy is on the total responsibility of the government officials to the expressed will curbed by constitutional individual rights. Nobody has a monopoly on the right answers. Therefore, there must be a constant open forum of dissenting views and opinions. Dissenting views are not only tolerated; they are needed and encouraged. Jefferson said: **"If there be any among us who would wish to dissolve this union or change its republican form, let them stand undisturbed as monuments of the safety with which error of opinion may be tolerated where reason is left free to combat it."**

3—Accent on the "select" community vs. accent on equality. In a democracy, the accent on the individual and his inviolable rights rules out any concept of a "select" community which would exclude anyone. The Declaration of Independence puts it simply: **"All men are born equal."** That is to say, they have equal rights in the community, no matter what their ancestry, race, religion, politics or economic station.

4—Accent on politics as religion vs. accent on conscience. Democracies have moral rules and impose certain of those moral rules by law. But these rules do not flow from any single state-supported theory—religious, philosophical, or political. They are arrived at by a consensus of the population. And, most important, the population has arrived at their moral and religious convictions *through their own various private beliefs and sources.* The democratic state scrupulously avoids meddling with these sources. In this sense, there exists what Jefferson called the "separation of church and state." The state does not prescribe religion, does not favor one religion over another, does not interfere with private religion in any way, or penalize anyone because of his religion.

The typical totalitarian techniques are, of course, out of keeping in the democratic society because they are all designed to manipulate the individual, and therefore downgrade his importance as an individual. But they are also less *usable* in a democratic society. Scapegoating becomes less feasible because it is invariably based on falsehood, and in a democratic society, falsehood can be publicly challenged. Double talk and The Big Lie are less usable for the same reasons. A government official can lie and twist meanings only at his own risk. His opponents will feel free to challenge him, and will have channels open to do so. The democratic state depends on its emotional appeal, but cannot afford to stress the emotional at the expense of the intellectual. Ideas and programs are subject to constant scrutiny, challenge, and dissent. Democracy depends on reflective debate to help increase emotional commitment. The totalitarian state depends on emotional commitment to help limit reflective debate.

The Appeal of Totalitarianism

The twentieth century, with its clumped populations, its high level of organization, its mass media of communications, advanced technology and emphasis on mass movements is ripe for totalitarianism—or for expanding democracy. These are the two basic ideologies that face each other in the world today.

At the moment, they face each other on the international scene in the form of communist totalitarianism versus "western" democracy. In the early part of the century it was a common illusion that communism represented primarily a form of economy, and that the debate was between communism and capitalism. Perhaps there was—and is—a legitimate economic debate as between forms of socialism and forms of capitalism. But as an economic system, the Soviet Union has some aspects of traditional socialism and some aspects of traditional capitalism; so has Great Britain. However, one nation is totalitarian in its accents and the other is democratic. It is not primarily a debate about economics in which the world is gripped—but a more fundamental debate about the total relationship of man to his society.

It is not yet known whether the perpetuation of power built into totalitarianism means that it can never change from within. There have been recurrently flickering hopes that internal circumstances might ease such communist countries as the Soviet Union into more flexible directions. It is apparent to most people that the totalitarian accents of Communist Poland, for example, are relatively less severe than those of Communist China. However, the significance of these apparent variations, if any, is not yet clear.

Meanwhile, totalitarianism is the issue—and totalitarianism of every stripe—communist, a new Nazism, or any other—is built on the same basic theory and has the same basic effect on the daily lives of the people. Some authors have projected the possibility of a future in which two huge totalitarian societies face each other in the world. But it is a basic fallacy to suppose that it takes totalitarianism to resist totalitarianism. Such a defense would obviously be self-defeating as far as democracy is concerned. It would make as much sense as committing suicide in order to prevent being killed.

And, desirability aside, there is no reason to suppose that a totalitarian society is more efficient in the long run than a democratic society. The ultimate failure of Hitler and the near failure of Stalin belie totalitarianism's claims to greater efficiency. Behind totalitarianism's façade of super-organization lies a vast waste of human resources.

Totalitarianism, then, is not just an international issue. Much of the national debate in democratic countries is concerned with the problem of the rights of the individual versus the rights of the state. Nazism went to the most extreme limits in its emphasis on: 1) *community* as against the individual; 2) *authority* as against expressed will; 3) *"select" community* as against equality; 4) *politics as religion* as against individual conscience. The first two contrasts are, of course, not absolutes but matters of strong emphasis. A democratic society needs a sense of community, but the central focus is always the individual. A democratic society needs leaders who can exert authority, but always within the strict limits of an operating responsibility to the people who elected them.

Besides these four broad measures against which issues can be gauged on the totalitarian-democratic scale, there are the warning signs revealed by Nazi techniques: the attempt to depreciate the intellect and reason; the attempt to manipulate people with glittering words—words such as "democracy" where democracy is not intended, "patriotism" where patriotism is not intended, "peace" where peace is not intended; and the use of scapegoating in any form. If there is a lesson in Nazism, it lies in its clear enunciation of these danger signals of totalitarianism. And it is a lesson which the citizens of free nations can ill afford to forget.

Totalitarianism obviously has a certain appeal for many people in the hard-pressed twentieth century. It sweeps aside increasingly complex problems, and offers simple answers. It offers "strong" men on "white horses" to provide these answers. It promises food for the hungry, peace for the anxious, freedom for the oppressed, security for the unnerved, and dignity for the humiliated. But most of all, it promises power for the "average man," known in totalitarian parlance as "the people."

On the practical level, totalitarianism has demonstrated that it can deliver none of these promises. Because of its very nature, it is impossible for totalitarianism to deliver peace, dignity, or freedom. De-individualization, by definition, means de-humanization. As for the oft-promised power to "the people," someone has noted: "It is doubtful whether any tyranny can be worse than that exercised in the name of the sovereignty of the people." As far as Nazism is concerned, this is as fitting an epitaph as any. Nazism began by feeding on fears and hatreds. It was spread and maintained by brutality and lies. This in itself is enough to condemn any system. But it did not stop there. Nazism left a legacy of 25,000,000 dead— men, women and children. Often, fallen societies leave behind monuments which give future generations an indication of the character of that society. The symmetry and serenity of the Parthenon give us insight into the ideals of Greece. Nazism's monuments, left standing for all to see, are the now empty gas chambers and crematoria at Dachau and Buchenwald.

BIBLIOGRAPHY

ADL Staff, PROFILE OF COMMUNISM. ADL, N. Y., 1961.
  A guide to the history, aims, programs and strategy of Communism.

Arendt, Hannah, ORIGINS OF TOTALITARIANISM. Harcourt Brace, N. Y., 1961.
  The social and cultural beginnings of tyranny.

Blond, George, DEATH OF HITLER'S GERMANY. Pyramid Books, N. Y., 1954.
  Describes how the Nazis were defeated in 1945.

Bullock, Allan, HITLER, A STUDY IN TYRANNY. Harper and Row, N. Y., 1964.
  A psychological and historical study of Adolf Hitler from his youth to his death.

Clarke, Comer, EICHMANN: THE MAN AND HIS CRIMES. Ballantine Books, N. Y., 1960.
  A biography of Eichmann, the mass murderer of 6,000,000 Jews.

Frank, Anne, THE WORKS OF ANNE FRANK. Doubleday, Garden City, N. Y., 1959.
  Diary of a Jewish girl living under the Nazi terror; plus her short stories.

Friedman, Philip, THEIR BROTHERS' KEEPERS. Crown Publishers, N.Y., 1957.
  Story of Christian heroes and heroines who helped oppressed Jews escape the Nazi terror.

Greenberg, Martin, A SHORT HISTORY OF COMMUNISM. ADL, N. Y., 1964.
  A clearly written account of the evolution of Marxist-Leninist ideology and the development of Soviet Russia.

Harris, Whitney R., TYRANNY ON TRIAL. Southern Methodist University Press, Dallas, 1954.
  An account of the Nuremberg war crimes trials.

Lipset, Seymour Martin, POLITICAL MAN; THE SOCIAL BASES OF POLITICS. Doubleday & Co., N. Y., 1959.
  Why men in society organize politically.

Manvell, Roger & Fraenkel, Heinrich, DR. GOEBBELS: HIS LIFE AND DEATH. Simon & Schuster, N. Y., 1960.
A biography of the Nazi propaganda minister.

Neumann, Franz, BEHEMOTH: THE STRUCTURE AND PRACTICE OF NATIONAL SOCIALISM. 1933-44. Oxford Press, N. Y., 1944.
How the Nazi system functioned, socially, politically and economically.

Neumann, Peter, BLACK MARCH: PERSONAL STORY OF AN SS MAN. Wm. Sloane Assoc., N. Y., 1958.
The training and personality of a Gestapo officer.

THE PERSECUTION OF THE CATHOLIC CHURCH IN THE THIRD REICH. Longmans, Green & Co., N. Y., 1940.
Describes the methods the Nazis used to subdue the Catholic Church in Germany.

Poliakov, Leon, HARVEST OF HATE. Syracuse University Press, Syracuse, N. Y., 1954.
Describes the Nazi program for the destruction of the Jews.

Robinson, Jacob and Friedman, Philip, GUIDE TO JEWISH HISTORY UNDER NAZI IMPACT. YIVO Institute for Jewish Research, N. Y., 1960.
An account of how the persecutions affected the Jews.

Roper, Edith and Leiser, Clara, NAZI JUSTICE. E. P. Dutton Co., N. Y., 1941.
Describes the perversion of justice by the Nazi government.

Rothfels, Hans, THE GERMAN OPPOSITION TO HITLER, AN ASSESSMENT. Oswald Wolff Publishers, Ltd., N. Y., 1961.
Provides the background to the German plot to assassinate Adolf Hitler and overthrow the Nazi government.

Russell, William, NAZI DOMINATED GERMANY. E. P. Dutton and Co., N. Y., 1941.
A description of the life of ordinary citizens in Nazi Germany.

Shirer, William, THE RISE AND FALL OF THE THIRD REICH. Simon & Schuster, N. Y., 1959.
A complete history of Nazi Germany.

Snyder, Louis L., HITLER AND NAZISM. Franklin Watt, Inc., N. Y., 1961.
A detailed account of how Hitler made the Nazi movement in his own image.

Co-sponsoring this publication with the Anti-Defamation League of B'nai B'rith is the Free Sons of Israel, the oldest national Jewish Fraternal Order in the United States, founded in 1849.

Through the communal service of this organization, generations of men, women and their children have found friendship and expression of love for America and its institutions. This organization is always ready to advance the principles of human equality, to help blot out oppression and to aid the weak. It has branches in New York, Miami, Chicago, Boston, Detroit and Los Angeles.